MURDER

MURDER

by

Michael Rothenberg

Paper Press

Michael Rothenberg
MURDER

Some of these poems have appeared previously in *Hoodoodog,
Otoliths, Apocrifa,* and *100 Thousand Poets for Change: An
International Anthology of Poetry* (Albeggi, Rome 2013).

Design, Layout, and Edited by Youssef Alaoui-Fdili

ISBN 10 0615839525
ISBN 13 978-0615839523

for Terri

MURDER

FEBRUARY 20

Murderous drug movie blood worm blooming crest,
convulsive quest of stars clot and spangle the fist, sleep,
wheeze, creased rubber sheet, blue lung of a boozy seraphim,
white squid and scrambled sweet bread, acid sputum brain
pan, pearls, grains, rains, verse, we give you our poems, our
songs, movies and comics and when it's time to pay for the
tears you want to sneak out the back door.

FEBRUARY 23

Invisible trombone combo, hippodrome, stone palindrome, homonym, anomaly, family tree.

Leaf blown off the deck into the moon.

Bloom, bone, rune, sewn, scar, fume, star, tune, serial disruption.

Mariachis on the wall of the many living waters.

Corridors of censure. Closure. Soldiers. Blood and oil wars. Boulders and skin, sloughed. Mechanisms of cacophony. Towers of rabble. Drivel, rubble, ruffle, dibble, dabble, rifle, riffle. Riff raff. Corn dogs and pollywogs.

A thrilling roller coaster ride breaks from its rolling tracks.

Dives, leaps, towards an astral attraction, across the zenith.

Of the living room.

Silver spoon. Destiny and coincidence.

You make the worst and most of your wayward dreams.

Gleeners, DNA, ecology, cataclysmic chaos and birth. Evolutionary dental floss, apology, string theory, calliope. Calliopic blues.

Love goes around the corner for a Margarita.

FEBRUARY 24: NATURAL DEATH

In Miami Beach in 1973, at a cocktail party at my next door neighbor's house, I heard that Buddy Zoloth, my brother's high school friend, had disappeared. His mother and father mingled at the party looking unusually sad as if life had lost all meaning. Rumor was that Buddy headed out west and died from an overdose and no one knew how to contact his family. Some friends thought maybe he was kidnapped and murdered. He just dropped off the face of the earth. His parents never heard from him again.

40 years later I see Buddy's picture on the Internet. He looks happy enough, reading a newspaper on a jet plane with Stephen Stills. He'd become a successful road manager in the 70's for several world famous Rock & Roll bands, including Manassas and Rita Coolidge. He seems to have had a nice loving family and was highly respected by his peers in the music industry. A legend.

But of course, shit does happen. Five years ago Buddy died from liver cancer at 59. Some say he deserved what he got but I'm not sure of that. I saw a comment like this on a memorial page online. He pissed off an ex-girlfriend or ex-wife. There was talk of guns and drugs and abuse. She was glad he was dead.

Interesting footnote is that last year someone found Buddy's address book from the 1970's while cleaning out a garage in LA. They tried to sell it for a "million dollars" to Pawn Stars, a television pawn shop program. But the telephone numbers for Neil Young, Grace Slick, Keith Richards, The Who and Elton John were no longer in service. So while this was a curious and compelling piece of memorabilia it was finally worthless. The Pawn Stars could find no buyers.

RIP Buddy. Good to hear you didn't disappear and die young. Though you didn't live very long. You just lived and died sooner or later like everyone else. But I wonder what happened to your parents.

*

The Weather Bureau predicts snow at sea level today or tomorrow. It's pretty fucking cold. I'm going to walk the dog.

FEBRUARY 25, 2011

The yellow motel with red shutters on the Hollywood Beach
Boardwalk, built in the 1940's, has a lovely view of white
sands and shimmering blue Atlantic waves, naked beer-
bellied Canadians slinging their pink dimpled guts across the
dunes. Somewhere beyond that is a teeming coral reef,
sharks, dolphins, sea turtles and a million billion sand
dollars. Maybe Cuba.

Weekly rates, daily rates, sun cream, coconut shampoo,
chocolates on the pillow at bedtime, beach towels & beach
chairs, hot tub, sauna, a tropical lounge on the patio beneath
the palms, Margaritas and Tequila Sunrise.

Jimmy Kanoodle, the bully boy probably from Madison,
Wisconsin walks around with a transistor radio plastered to
his ear.

I don't know where they got those bicycles but it sure looks
fun stuck to the seat in the sun, steering with one hand and a
frozen yogurt cone dripping in the other. Lick, pedal, lick,
pedal, crisp red blistering shoulders, white shorts and straw
hats, lick, pedal, lick, lick, watch out for the kid with the
purple plastic bucket and shovel, he shouldn't be running
with flippers on.

FEBRUARY 26, 2011

Black.

It never snowed last night. But there was ice on the road.
Gaddafi says, "Libya will be red with fire."

Irrelevant people have all the money.
You go to poetry school, get your poetry permit, your license
to practice.

(Permission to breathe).

*

*So what can a poor boy do/ Except to sing for a rock & roll
band/ Cause in sleepy London town there's no place for a
street fighting man.*

Rolling Stones sell MacDonald's breakfast sausage
sandwiches and recreational trucks. Record the soundtrack
for our Times while engineers rule the world.

Black.

But where I live the game to play is compromise solution.

*

Now what will you do with all your green, green money?
Gray blue money? Black and blue dollars and cents?

Diamonds and gold? Rose colored hundred dollar bills,
absolute yen, dissolute drachmas, and spangled lire?

*

Spyro Euros and spinach pie!

On the Heathrow runway ready to take off. The pilots are talking. "I'd like to invite you over to my house for a duck dinner."

Black Simoleons!

Gravity falls short of expectation.

*

REGRET

Have you ever thought of completing
one of those beautiful sunsets you began years ago
before you were widowed by alcohol and cancer?

*

CAUSE & EFFECT

"Raise the window please. It's much too windy for me back here. I've already got an earache."

FEBRUARY 27

Wedgewood plates with burgundy and black flowers, faded, cracked and stained.

One night when the dishes were still new I was building a Dagwood sandwich in the kitchen. My mother was in her bedroom watching late night TV. I carelessly dropped the dishes in the sink.

"Be careful with them," my mother shouted. "They're the last dishes I'll own in my life!" She got my attention. Suddenly, the China took on a life and death meaning.

And suppose the dishes survived her? What will my responsibility be to these prized and forlorn dishes? Will they be my last dishes too?

Photographs of dead uncles in the Jewish mob smoking fat cigars in silver suits. Zaftig aunts in pearls and mink stoles drinking fancy cocktails in a Philly speakeasy. Grandparents in modest bathing suits lounging on lawn chairs in the humid fresh cut green grass South Beach summer. And those unidentified military buddies, classmates, relatives and friends of the family posed beneath a palm tree, sharp and young, having fun, now stored in the wicker basket that belonged to my grandmother. "This was grandmas wicker basket," my mother told me. I made special note of that just in case it was ever important in the future, which is now. It's not an antique wicker basket, it's just old. Maybe she bought it at Woolworth's.

It was convenient all those years growing up to have everything taken care of for me. Family stories preserved in someone else's memory.

"What ever happened to those baseball cards?" My brother said. "They were worth a lot!" "Or those photographs I took." The old man in New York City sitting on a garbage can reading a newspaper with the headlines, "Nixon Reveals New Relief Plan." There's never been any relief yet. And that oversized and epic sepia portrait of a black man in beads and leather vest, American flag scarf around his head standing beside the white woman with frizzy hair and peasant blouse. A couple from the democratic multitudes caught in a prophetic glance. He had them framed and forgot about them for 40 years. "Those photos were really important!" My brother said.

Immaculate memories. Someone must look after them (if not look at them). I put them away for safe-keeping. This is what my mother taught me. But some things don't work out.

*

"In Episode 4 of *Who Do You Think You Are?* Kim Cattrall set out to discover what happened to her maternal grandfather after he disappeared 70 years ago, leaving his wife and daughters on their own in Depression-era Liverpool." She found out he was a bigamist. But who is Kim Cattrall? Do we care?

FEBRUARY 28: THE SOUND & COLOR DEPT. FOR JIM: BOOM! BANG! RED!

I want a new pair of pajamas without holes in the crotch.
A button or two would be fine, where they're supposed to be,
but it's not necessary.

Up in the mountains of Maine the provincial poet designs an
artificial brain for light and sound to circumambulate
reflection. But light and dark don't always go together with
commas and periods. The nuts and bolts of grammar tend to
reinforce our weaker habits.

You go wherever you go with whatever you wear and that
birch or sumac, bedraggled heart and triumphant conclusion
persists without fame or fortune.

It's almost Spring. Maybe another week of rain. The rose
bushes have begun to show their leaves. Rhododendron and
camellias swell with buds. The creek talks to the barking
dogs but the conversation is one-sided.

MARCH 1

Curly black fungus on the roadside. Rotted pine needles and soggy oak leaves in the dirt. The weather lady says it will rain all day and all week. But every afternoon my writing room fills up with sunshine. It's toasty and I like it. So bright and quiet. My sun.

MARCH 2

Roasted peanuts at 4pm when the sun drops in. Spider silk
floats between mind and cause. Whose voice is it that
straddles a patch of delirious daylight? You want me to
apologize? I don't have the patience for that kind of poetry.

MARCH 3: NEWS JUNKIE

1.

News junkie snorts the silver screen through electronic straw
and the holocaust narrative resumes. We're doing just fine
considering how bad things are going everywhere. Sanguine
shots, cold on the lips, warm as tears in the gut, intoxicates a
tabloid flood of pretty tits and ass. Oh, so, so, so sensation!

2.

Hooked on hooked, to see, buy, feel, fly at some safe
distance above the global wreckage. Watch it! Truth is
simple. It's one side or the other until there's a new other
side. Dig? Paradigms, dichotomies, phenomenologies, and
shadows. The forest doesn't tell me all I want to know so
I stay tuned to find out.

3.

That dead wood rat I saw on the road, Daily decimations,
fuzzy fungus and toads. All goes back to the earth. But
where does that shiny spirit, consciousness go? Out like a
light? Or does it join the broadcast news cavalcade? Become
part of the daily casualty parade, sports, hourly updates and
weather?

4.

Write it down! Every night a marching alibi at 7, 9 and 11.
I take a pill to fall asleep, my soporific entry to circumvent
the nighttime questioning terrors. To turn off the broadcast
entertainment of rising fame and falling stars. But the pill
dissolves and dreams resolve to blog and post the disjunctive
embroidery, tablet, stele, rune. . .

5.

The bilious broadcast continues. I walk down zombie streets
scattered with trash and light. I enter an abandoned building.
Follow squeaking stairs into a basement strewn with beams
and plaster. I discover a shimmering pool under the debris.
I climb in and sink below the mirrored surface. I swim
through the monotone unknown and can only guess what I'm
imagining.

It's 6 pm or 1 am. I swim and swim. What happens next?
The news takes me home.

(S&CD: Crack. Gurgle, gurgle. Blue)

MARCH 4: CHEESE for Jack Collom

The abbreviated condition. Grilled chicken and cheese.
Democracy! Winter rains all over again. Spring stumbling
around in soggy garden. Pink clover blossoms.

An appointment. She shoves a small round mirror in
my mouth to see the back of my teeth. Sibilance. I heard you
call. My gums recede. Ups and downs. I'm going
somewhere again. Looney tunes! Clean the yard. Golden
centipedes in the rotted wood pile. Don't touch that! Nature.

Looking on the bright side. It's all good. Nurture. The results
are clearly mixed. I saw the sun now I'm waiting for
a cheese enchilada to deliver me. Longhand. As if. If so.
Therefore. Chocolate chip cookies and Bollywood. *Swades*.
A great movie but terrible translation.

Now back to the motherland. A small town were we loved
each other for eternity. Our hands move over that cluttered
curve. Enough! It's a better world for inactivity.

MARCH 5: TWEET

Who cares what stars do!
So far away in Hollywood

Blah
Blah

Obelisk
Oblique

Noblesse oblige

Don't count
On it

MARCH 5: REDUX

Goodbye, polar bears!
Climate strange
Where do we go from here?
We're in for trouble
The two of them against the five us, makes seven
A lucky number
Wilson Pickett!
Scratch that or bet the Daily Double
Charlie Sheen is the winner
Poor guy...
Who is the Lindsay Lohan of Poetry?
I'd like to follow her tweets
And why not?
I've got some unfinished business
in this nasty jungle.

MARCH 5: "I'M TWITTERING!"

Spring is in the air
And what about those people you know
Ripping you off?
"Are white people afraid of life?" (Terri)
Before I patent it, I'll google it
Oh, Infinite Monkey!

MARCH 6

It's a dark & fuzzy day. Love is difficult. Generally. I saw a 5
hr movie, *Jodhaa Akbar* (Aishwarya Rai & Hrithik Roshan)
– "Khwaja." This song blew me away.

LOST IN SPACE

Disassociating. Lost in space. Abused and alcoholic mother.
Deepest apologies to Neeli. I rarely forget an appointment.
I have one now with Jonathan about ecopoetics and the oil
spill in the Gulf of Mexico. An alcoholic son. Sexist. Racist,
failing statistics. Remember that? And on Tuesday I meet
with Don The Handyman. He's an okay guy. Coming to fix
a hole in the wall and put up a towel rack up in the guest
bathroom. Overbearing, emotional, loud, needy, a recovering
alcoholic. He's going to do it for cheap. How could I forget
that? On Wednesday night I meet Brian to talk about Philip
Whalen, walk through Philip's robes and count his ivory
beads. Fish Drum! Klunk. Klunk. I'm not running with any
particular crowd these days. (Or ever). The Queen Enabler!
And don't forget those formative years in Alabama with
uncles drinking and shooting. That's when we got
divorced...HONK!

*

Bristly, thorny, shacked up with a porn star, too busy
twittering to get laid. Countering inhumanity one joint
at a time. I'm not impressed with most people.
Glitch. Bitch. Bitch.

Saved by Bollywood!

MARCH 7: ON THE BRIGHT SIDE OF LOVE

French fries. Gulf oil disaster wasn't a complete waste.
Hollywood "got a movie out of it…" Can't wait for *Revenge
of The Fracker! Oil Blob. Attack of The Six-Headed Shrimp.
The Bloody Lung of Plaquemines Parish.*

Cuban coffee loaded with cream and sugar. A call from my
son. Terri's laughter. Ziggy and Puma! Sunlight, oceans,
mountains, creeks, rivers, bugs. The consoling torrent of rain
in the redwoods. Fourteen redwood trees cut down for a
lawn so puppies and babies can roll around. Nimby me?
Twist and shatter of broken scenes. Turkey, ham, tomatoes
and cucumber on sourdough French with Thousand Island
dressing. Night's impossible angle. Confused cuckoo
clocks. Things happen too quickly in the morning. It takes
me a while to get going. At last, the dental assistant rejoins
with firehouse and cattle prod.

Greasy pizza by the slice in Hollywood, Florida. What I do
with my day and judgment of wage slaves. Who do I belong
to? Truth slaughtered in cerulean geographies.

Gorgeous blue moth. Radiant jellyfish. Salutary pink worm.
Cameo. Romeo. It takes a week to write three words.
Electronic Velcro. But I can't remember the third. Smoke
and tears in cadaver's subdural attic. You take a bus there.
Get off anywhere. You can always get back on again for free
if you save the stub. I get the senior's discount at Food For
Humans. The dybbuk's incandescent howl. Petro-pimps and
Backhoes.

Vanilla yogurt sprinkled with pumpkin seed and raisin
granola. I have a fear of zoos. A fear of one food touching
another. Fear of contradictions and phobias. Enough!
Enough! I have a fear of poetry by Jewel and Maya Angelou.

Pillsbury Dough Boy and Speedy Alka-Seltzer. I'm eternally retro! Link one oozing disease to another. Humility always as tough as nails to sell. It fits like a barbed wire glove. Shameless self-loathing is a naked empire without cheeseburgers.

On the bright side of love.

It's good for the cows. Farewell, Human Zoo! Farewell, God!

MARCH 10

Oprah Magazine features "Eight poets - accessorized with snippets of their own verse celebrate freedom of expression…" An "unapologetically political spoken-word artist in a $395 striped tank top…"

"Lopsided, rheumy, bile-ridden, sweet, spiritual, wormy and demented. All going down in a body to paint the steeple pure and bright." *Black Spring*, Henry Miller.

If I live long enough it will all make sense. But I never will. No one does.

*

The camellias opened today.
Pink!

MARCH 11: RELIQUARY TSUNAMI for PW

Does being an artist mean you just make "art"? Or is it
something more than that? Like The Weavers! Or "Dear
Mr. President" et. al.? Oh, Lady Gaga? Raised to sainthood,
she breaks off negotiations with Target, dons a meatloaf
shroud and crawls on her knees to the top of the Hollywood
Hills.

The racist pundit? What can be done with him? Jowls flap
over the airwaves. In last throes of his wretched anagrams,
parallelograms, charts, graphs, bile and bluster. Put the car
in reverse, back over him, hair peace and Oxycontin,
all of it, crush him beneath the fiery wheel. Don't worry, he's
already wounded beyond surgery or prayer. Put him
out of his misery. Put him in a 50 gallon drum and bury him
at Bitburg Cemetery. Art or artifact? Just put a label on it:
"On Donation from the Private Collection of the Koch
Brothers."

Zendo. Oh, Zendo. Oh, lend me your ears!

Whoosh.

I'm going to Santa Rosa, California to see the Philip Whalen
Artifacts.

Credit ratings. Camel humps. Swizzle sticks in the sand.
"Word Ocean." Seashells, pink murex, triton horn, and
tsunami. On the way back down you follow the lineage.
Cheez-its left by Hansel and Spike Jones. Dolmas.
Chrysanthemum of Spanish cheeses. Mixed exotic olives
from the ruins of Mediterranean Europe. Saki. Saki. Protests
in Wisconsin. A State of Emergency. The Poetry
Corporation.

"You load sixteen tons, and what do you get?/another day older and deeper in debt/St. Peter, don't you call me, 'cause I can't go/I owe my soul to the company store." The Go-Go version.

Flowers like rain all day long. Red Wine. Raksu. Chop. "Dear Mr. President." Earthquake and tsunami in Japan. "Lady Gaga designs Japan earthquake relief wristwatch."

Walk down the broken streets. Nothing belongs to anyone. A fishing trawler in aisle 11 at Ishinomaki Costco. The planet has gone noodles. Zafu. Snafu. Bok choy. Death radish shuffle. That kinked and wrinkled tube of impermanent glue. Apply to the surface of anything that once was precious, or beautiful. Each keepsake. Perfect oneness. The gravy in my beard refuses to stick. Brain rot. Brainiac. Brain candy. Celebrex. Kerouac. Pick up the phone and call Basho. Contemplation on the line. Talk over catholic enlightenment and vendetta's dystopic polarity.

10,000 people have perished so far. It's always perfect. "We shall overcome." A man adrift on roof of his house swept out to sea. 200,000 people evacuated. "I have every confidence in ourselves." Shogun. Caveat chariot. My brain is going to break. Perfect. Prefect. Partial Fukushima meltdown. Brain pan. Brain coral. Total meltdown. Sea water enema to cool rods. "There are contradictory reports so we really don't know what the fuck is going on." A sea of mud, wool hats, shoes, brainstems, automobiles, begging bowls and calorie counters.

Stupa. Santa Rosa reliquary. Rosary. Ring of bones. People will come see the change purse, ceremonial flute, calligraphy, nibs and sumi brush, thick glasses, and the little talking box, he used to push the button that tells the time out loud. A lady's voice. Asleep. Shrine. Acrimony and forgiveness. Sublime religious suite. They'll come and meditate, celebrate with all their contradictions and frailties, pride and prejudice, the good, pink round man and his divine morning incense.

"If I wasn't drunk & blowing wine-fumes & peanut breath in your face maybe you'd be nice to me."

MARCH 13

O beautiful madrone! O, beautiful rain! I like it here in
Guerneville.

I'm kind of a hippy. Yes, I burn incense. When I'm out of
breath it helps me catch my breath. Obsessions go up in
smoke.

A pneumonic device. O, yes. Like Bells. O, yes, I remember
them both. The bells and incense. Remember it all.
Obsessions. Midnight forests drenched in white moonlight.
Flowers and sunlight. Daylight Savings Time. Woohoo!

On the roof deck I smoke a bowl of Northern California pot.
Here comes the wisteria! The buds are fat and all over the
place. I don't see the difference between a Jew and
a Buddhist. I'm neither one of them, or both. It's like having
a squirrel and a marching brass band in your head. Religion.
Phooey!

O, beautiful rain! Beautiful madrone!
O, rosy Calypso orchid splash in the mush.
Sip some mango juice. Imagine Japan.
Poor Japan.

MARCH 14: .WHAT I TOLD HIM

What's going on? Is it the end?

"We will be saved, only with the birth of a new and militant radicalism which seeks to dethrone our corrupt elite from power, not negotiate for better terms." – Chris Hedges

.
It seems clear that three of them reactors are out of control, right? So where is the president? When do they get on TV and tell us not to worry?

I call my congresswoman to ask her what is going on! I tell her she should send out a newsletter or something!

"Dear Friends, In case you think it's the end of the world, I thought I'd drop you a line to say howdy! Don't worry about radiation. Just go seal yourself indoors and don't come out until I tell you to."

We hire these politicians to do shit for us that doesn't end up meaning anything, while daily life murders us. I wonder what General Electric is doing today, or BP?

All of these mother fucking murderers. We've got a front row in the theater of our own extinction.

.
I hear Mars is beautiful. "That's where I'm gonna go when I die." Venus might be beautiful too! I'd like to read some more Kenneth Patchen and Henry Miller. I wonder if they're both still writing on Mars?

MARCH 15

Charlie Sheen trumped by Japanese earthquake, tsunami,
and nuclear disaster? Sloth, despair, mesmerized by
technology…I don't want your fucking technology!

It's extremely gloomy today. I like it when it rains but there's
a lot of bad news today. I feel claustrophobic.

"Open the window."

My best friend Jim is having a nervous breakdown
in Santa Rosa.

It's difficult to equivocate. "Little Murders."
Hiroshima on the rocks. I gave up drinking for what?
America on radiation alert.

By the time you read this I'll be walking the dog in
radioactive rain but don't worry. Scientists say, "texting"
while driving is more dangerous.

Vampires or nuclear reactors?
Choose your medicine.
Sodium iodide.

MARCH 16: FOODIES

"And pancakes every morning of the world."

That's not such a bad thing. Green tea and toast?
Nope, give me pancakes slathered in maple syrup!

Laundry. Dishes. Listen to news.

"Don't give up hope," says the Emperor of Japan.

"We've got it under control," says the Tokyo Electric
Power Company.

"Lock yourself indoors and don't come out until we tell
you," the Japanese president says.

"…all energy sources have downsides and none are
foolproof, " Obama says.

He's got 36 billion dollars in his budget for incentives to
expand nuclear power industry. 30 billion in subsidies for
the oil industry. I'm sure he'll get re-elected in 2050.

Humans are short-sighted, stupid and greedy. Did you ever
see a windmill meltdown? Is it silly for me to imagine
a solution?

No, I will not shut up and leave management of the planet
to brighter people than myself.

"And pancakes every morning of the world."

I've got a sweet tooth at 11pm. Something natural and fluffy!
Death by chocolate.

Or a midnight mushroom and onion pizza, bourbon on the rocks in bed where no one can find me. So much for a green fucking economy.

"Horrors of biblical proportion" unfold and we wonder why!

Liar, liar, radioactive pants on fire!

I want maple syrup with real maple syrup in it. I'm tired of crying...

NEWS UPDATE FUKISHIMA:

"Bay Area foodies may be inconvenienced by the lack of sushi in the days to come."

MARCH 18: APOLOGY REDUX

It's hard to look away.

Torn limbs, broken toys, what could have been a house is a lump of pick up sticks in a political game.

"Irreversible technological insanity."

Put a gun to your head and blame the weather.

All day long. . .

How many times can I sing about blue jays?

In the face of an incomprehensible disaster, instead of celebrating poetry you hide. Why is that? Don't you trust poetry?

Why do I write?

It's a nervous twitch and I wasn't loved as a child…

MARCH 21

I know the names but not the sad, sad mistaken faces. Count
them. Pale plastic shells, hallowed shards, blunt-edged
puzzle pieces, dioramic snapshots. Count them. Reach
myopic odyssey. Fabulous sideways fiction. Climb on board.
Sign them in. Count them. Saintly numbers. Multitudes.
Walt! Yeah, Karaoke Multitudes...

He's a real bad dog (not a real dog) and this wanna be hound
wants to shit on our velvet roses. Wants his balls scratched
all fucking daylong, barks and whines to be taken out at 2am
so he can piss on himself. He's an absolute digression.

While one more oil soaked coral wilts in vertigo of yellow
moonlight, glorious flower hacks its petals into desolate fall,
20 thousand Rockhopper penguins burst into acid flames on
Tristan Da Cunha Islands, another benzene starlight plume
seeps and scars an oceanic paradise...

I hear them cry, folks on the Gulf of Mexico Coast. Bubbly
white rashes head to toe, spit up grit and blood, shout about
jobs. Not enough of them jobs! I hope they understand what
they've signed up for. Corporate slavery toiling in the
bowels of extinction. Howl on you bloody petroleum slaves.
I love you but as far as I can see there's nothing I can do to
help.

Sad faces in rain. Sushi foodies. Pacifist trolls garden the last
sustainable feast of plutonium lettuce, pedigreed bok choy
and electric radishes. Gardeners, I admire your cultured
pacifism, yes, but you move too slowly in your haiku.

Is this where the massacre continues? Sociopathic
brainwaves. Diastolic embolisms. Is it positive change?

Is it any kind of change? Should poetry and politics mix or be kept separate, like urine and strawberries, as if politics were something else besides what we've become, or what we believe in, or who we are?

REDACT

Sure, Death, I understand
You have a bad cancer

Agoraphobic, paralyzed
Broke, starved

Dissolute and wasted
It's no joke

Salmonella in the driveway
and I can't get it started

MARCH 22: STOP. START

Sleepers Awake.

Rake rotted log chunks into a pile. Shovel them into the blue
wheelbarrow. Shove debris over the side of the hill into the
forest of silver oaks. Nobody will know the difference.
Go inside. Take off my wool hat and gloves. Grab a handful
of granola and go upstairs to check e-mail. Think about
100 Thousand Poets for Change.

Click. Click.
Share. Click.
Send.

I wait indoors for winter to end mostly distracted by bad
news, that's what retired people do. Make regular trips to the
kitchen to satisfy a constant hunger, stay away from
chocolate chip cookies and stupidly run out of propane.
I order a refill. They tell me it will take one to seven days for
delivery unless I want to pay a special delivery fee of 150
dollars. I'll wait. Conserve. Use space heaters. The hot water
is electric.

A break in the clouds.

Terri sighs. It wakes the dog up.
Translation?
Click. Click. Share. Click.
Make new friends.
Click.

The propane delivered but the line is full of air.

Stop.

Toast a slab of blueberry muffin and dip it in butter.

Start.

I hear there's a leak in the reactor core at Fukushima.
It seems I've heard that before. Radiation clouds as far away
as Sweden and United States of America.

Stop. Start.

Do they use mops in those other two billion earth-like
planets in this galaxy? Domesticity is endangered. Rabid
vacuum cleaners murder each other in town square.

Stop.

At the San Diego Zoo there's an 1800 acre wildlife preserve
houses over 3500 different household cleaners representing
260 brands, 100 manufactures, and it's also a botanical
garden.

Start.

A one-eyed, all purpose kitchen sponge with no mouth dies
in an India incubator.

I've attached a Geiger counter to my pillow to detect
radioactive dreams and other paranoid redundancies.

Stop. Start.

MARCH 28: HELL OR HIGH WATER

Plutonium in the tunnel. It's the 28th. What does that mean?
Nothing. Come hell or high water. The two headed dolphin
with electronic squeakers goes to warn settlers. *Lysistrata.*
She bounces a basketball down the street, followed by a
disobedient chain saw. Foul! The basket is suspended from
Bilbao. A bouquet of bananas. Only two of them are real.
The other one is Ezra Pound.

*

Toothpick. Pink gums. Sea serpents. Poppy seeds. Lime
scale.

APRIL 2

Change?

Grilled ham & cheese with pickles
Can you remember that?

Organization?

The ocean is a human toilet
Sigh and bitch

Anarchy?

I envy a banana slug

APRIL 14

A wolf in forget-me-nots!

APRIL 21: THE GARDEN

Bright green maple leaves

Pink Camellia
Purple Wisteria

Yellow and black bumble bees
In the redwoods

APRIL 29

Sad poets do their dance
Ira Cohen wasn't a sad poet
Has anybody seen Spain?

MAY 2: GREEN AMMO

Ira Cohen Obituary in New York Times
The same day Obama announces the death of Osama Bin
Laden. Ira would have loved that fact

'Green' Ammo: Army To Demonstrate Lead-Free
Ammunition

We need green mines, green daisy cutters,
green nuclear warheads, green
assault rifles, green generals, green soldiers,
green hand grenades, green amputees,
green widows, green coffins... a perfect world
A sustainable war!

Now I'm waiting for morning in Beirut
May 10, the phone rings at the Ministry of Culture
A poet in California is looking for 100 Thousand Poets for
Change in Lebanon

MAY 2: LEBANON CALLING

It's difficult dealing in so many languages
Everyone struggles to communicate
Many use a Google Translator
or other electronic translators that hardly make sense
I had an impossible conversation with a very nice woman
from the Ministry of Culture in Lebanon
They speak Arabic there. I don't
After an awkward exchange of broken starts and stops
there was nothing she could do but hang up on me
So I went and found her email online and wrote her a letter
She wrote back and apologized for her English
And explained because of political situations
they couldn't do anything about peace or sustainability
in Lebanon right now...

*

We used to talk about souls
Some bird and fire strained towards eternity
But the earth is flat and atmosphere shrinking
It's impossible to talk to anyone anymore
or die with grace

*

On a farm in North Dakota
reading to blackbirds and stars
some message of change. I thought I heard

A choir of politicians sing, "DRILL, BABY, DRILL!"

MAY 19

I heard from a poet who said he was not interested in the 100 Thousand Poets for Change initiative because he didn't want to undermine the Obama administration. He thought it could be picked up by the wrong people...

MAY 19: FOREST NEWS

63 freedomfighters
Shot dead in Damascus

Orange butterfly wings
Pulse on the doormat

A reckless dawn
Hangs on the garden fence

Like a broken bird
There is no truth

Only an itch behind the knee
Beneath ashen leaves

The squirm and twitch
Of smoke in sweet rain

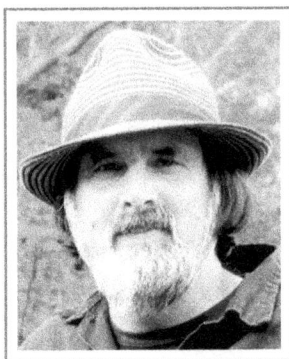

Michael Rothenberg is a poet, songwriter, editor and publisher of the online literary magazine Big Bridge, www.bigbridge.org and co-founder of the global poetry movement 100 Thousand Poets for Change.

His editorial work includes several volumes in the Penguin Poets series: *Overtime* by Philip Whalen, *As Ever* by Joanne Kyger, *David's Copy* by David Meltzer, and *Way More West* by Ed Dorn. He is also editor of *The Collected Poems of Philip Whalen* published by Wesleyan University Press.

Rothenberg's book of poems, *Indefinite Detention: A Dog Story* is scheduled for publication in 2013 by Ekstasis Editions, Victoria, B.C., Canada and in 2014 by both Shabda Press (USA) and Al Kotob Khan (Cairo, Egypt) in an Arab/English edition, translated by El Habib Louai.

ALSO BY MICHAEL ROTHENBERG

- *The Paris Journals* (Fish Drum Press)

- *Man/Women*, with Joanne Kyger (Big Bridge Press)

- *Choose* (Big Bridge Press)

- *Unhurried Vision* (La Alameda/University of New Mexico Press)

- *My Youth As A Train* (Foothills Publishing)

- *Favorite Songs* (Big Bridge Press)

- *Punk Rockwell* (Tropical Press)